*The universe is*
*one vast glimmer*
*of light –*

*mirrored*
*in a sunbeam…*

Published in the United Kingdom by Sundara Poetry Press.



Cover design by C.W. Blackburn

ISBN: 978-1-7397728-2-6

# ONE HUNDRED COLOURS OF BEING

*Poems in the Spirit of Zen*

C.W. Blackburn

Sundara Poetry Press

*For the benefit of all beings,*
*in full measure, without exception.*

*Through the merit of our practice,*
*may we attain, in loving kindness –*
*the great, natural peace.*

# *Foreword*

In its highest form, poetry is the art of constructing a doorway from the mundane to the essential. It achieves this by giving as much respect to pauses as to words, to breaks as to punctuation and to the unspoken as to the spoken. The reader is invited to participate, to *feel* rather than understand and to touch, even if for a brief moment, something universal. Each of C.W. Blackburn's poems in this book, his third collection, is such a doorway or invitation into our shared being.

Whenever and wherever in the world men and women experienced the mystical depths of being, the ecstasy of love or the beauty of the imperishable Truth, they reached for the poetic form as a vehicle to convey a glimpse of their experience. Yet the writers of such sublime poetry, whether they were Zen monks, Christian mystics, *bhakti* saints, or the *Sufis*, did not identify themselves as poets; they were simply like flowers that had bloomed, from whom poetry flowed out as a sweet fragrance. As C.W. writes, 'No-one ever told me / I could call myself a poet – / but whose permission do I need / to celebrate / existence?'

In a hundred succinct poems reminiscent of the Japanese *tanka* style, C.W. explores the 'One Hundred Colours of Being' by diving deep into his own experience and returning with insights and sharings that are eminently relatable. Carrying the spirit of the Zen tradition, with their patient pacing, simplicity and metaphor, each of the five-line poems is a little invitation to the reader to pause, be present and savour the meditativeness and subtle understanding from which the words emerge. Typically in Zen poetry, one receives a sense of the poet's experience in which the present moment is considered as one totality – oneself and whatever else makes up the present moment, is all there is. 'Just this'. From the realisation of this unified ground of being, arise utterances that make fresh connections between the apparent objects of perception and oneself, in order to point to or celebrate that oneness. 'The sound of water says what I think', the Chinese philosopher, Zhuangzi, so delightfully penned.

This is to say that when the inner seeing opens up in us, then though the objects of our perception are just as they have always been, they are now *seen* differently. As William Blake described it, it is 'To see a World in a Grain of Sand / And a Heaven in a Wild Flower, / Hold Infinity in the palm of your hand / And Eternity in an hour.' C.W. Blackburn's poems embody such a sensitivity and subtlety of perception. Imagery from nature is frequently woven into the poems and placed alongside expressions of personal experience, evoking a sense of the unity of being. In one place he writes, 'This butterfly flits by – / shimmering its colour, / and shining starlight in my eyes. / Oh, through this heart-felt connection – / we're one and the same.'

As has been noted by sages, saints and seers over the centuries, as we evolve in consciousness, the way we use language changes. Words and sound have indeed always held an important place in spirituality. India's Vedic tradition speaks about cosmic sound and vibrations and different subtleties of *vak* or speech (corresponding to the Latin, *vox*) while the Bible too conveys the primordial nature of the 'Word' ('In the beginning was the Word, and the Word was with God, and the Word was God' – John 1:1). As our limited structures of self and old ways of perceiving and relating with the world dissolve, the vibrations of sound or thought that issue forth from us, come differently arranged. In spiritual or mystic poetry, this aspect is of paramount importance. Words arranged by Presence look, sound and *feel* different to words that come from a mind heavily laden with beliefs and personal identity.

And herein lies the real power of spiritual poetry – to elevate the mind and consciousness of the reader through words chosen and arranged from a place of connection with the Whole. In this way, the reader receives a taste of the universal power that works through all things, largely in invisible and subtle ways. 'What abundance / is at work behind these words? / Only the same force / that turns the ripening summer wheat / into gold', chimes one poem in this book.

C.W. Blackburn's unpretentious and honest voice is refreshing in a genre where one may tend to veer towards flowery proclamations of love and bliss and forget to mention the pain overcome along the path. Another challenge of the genre of spiritual poetry is that an excitement to share one's spiritual experience can quite easily force one's hand instead of patiently allowing the words to form themselves and the flow arising from within to take the lead. Only when quietly seated in the neutrality of being, can something of the *essence* pour forth.

It is gladdening to see a revival of interest in poetry in our present times and especially to see poets like C.W. Blackburn sharing the depths of their experience in the vein of mystic seers of ancient times. While connoisseurs of literary poetry may lament the short attention spans of modern-day readers, reflected also in the brevity of expression encouraged by social media channels like Twitter or Instagram, it may be noted that the poets of the Zen tradition or the sutra writers of the Vedic or Buddhist traditions have long revelled in the ability to speak volumes, indeed to convey the most profound experiences and wisdom, through only a few words or lines. Unlike in other genres of poetry where one might admire or wonder at the poet's skill at putting together the words, as you go through the poems in this book, you might rather like to ponder, *from where is the poet speaking these words?*

As is often said on the spiritual path, the question is more important than the answer. The Zen tradition says: we do not find answers but at some point, the questions dissolve. Gently holding this inquiry into the source of the words as we read C.W. Blackburn's poems, may just deliver us to the place of his speaking, where the questioning dissolves – into our very own being.

***Shruti Bakshi***
Author of *HeartWords: Mystic Poems*
Founder of the LivingWise Project
India, August 2022

(i.)

This life is like a flower,
cast adrift upon the sea.

On the furthest shore,
there is a stranger who will find it,
and help it to grow.

(ii.)

What is this world to us
but a changing season?
A dream of springtime colour –

carried here by the wind,
and just as soon forgotten.

(iii.)

As I heal old wounds,
I feel my breath grow deeper.

Oh, what a miracle it is –
this incredible lightness
of being.

(iv.)

When my heart feels regret,
I yearn to turn back time.

What a relief then when I realise –
each star is guided
by a singular motion.

(v.)

What solace could I ever
hope to find in this weary,
broken heart?

The same love I cling to
brings the colour to the leaves.

(vi.)

I don't want to keep making
the same old mistakes.

When they flower in spring,
the blossoms don't remember
the darkness of winter.

(vii.)

There's a lifetime held
in the blinking of an eye.

Watch as it happens –
as one world ends,
a whole universe opens.

(viii.)

What abundance
is at work behind these words?

Only the same force
that turns the ripening summer wheat
into gold.

(ix.)

All our love is held in a single note –
so why hide from that joy?

Even the sparrows call out lightly
as they mate beneath
a stainless sky.

(x.)

Throwing stones into the sea
I watch the ripples fade away.

As my dreams disappear
into this thousandfold world –
they come back to me in kind

(xi.)

Though I am often told
to take heed of all my faults –
my second sight keeps telling me:

I'm worth the weight
of heaven.

(xii.)

Whilst others search for answers,
I turn my mind
towards this question:

in a world of such division,
what is the colour of our being?

(xiii.)

All of life is a dance!
There's no-one that stands still
in this space that surrounds me –

only the wind that comes and goes,
as I release another breath.

(xiv.)

I went outside this morning
to listen to the flowers.

Closing my eyes amongst
the newly opened roses, I heard the footfalls
of distant angels.

(xv.)

How tender the words
that capture the subtle elegance
of the cherry blossoms –

expressing life's beauty
just as it is.

(xvi.)

As we pour more wine,
my eyes become heavy.

Don't give me too much,
or I'll start spouting my wisdom!

Let's drink from the same cup.

(xvii.)

Sometimes the air gets so close
I feel like I can't breathe.

It's hard to remember
what the fear makes me forget:

this body is a gift.

(xviii.)

The stones
have endured their lot
for a time I can't fathom.

Still I get restless
for some kind of change.

(xix.)

Even this despair
is a part of the unity
I am grateful for.

Stretching beyond my limits,
I take refuge in surrender.

(xx.)

The incense's smoke
fills the air with its aroma,
and disappears just as quickly.

Ah, but beyond the mist,
the fragrance remains.

(xxi.)

Blue mountains cannot hide
from the autumn wind. Look –
in the pine trees, a hundred Buddhas appear!

When I close my eyes on this world,
the dreaming simply stops.

(xxii.)

I can't stop imagining
all these things that I desire.

I don't want to renounce anything!

Oh, if only I had the room for it,
I'd buy the very sunset.

(xxiii.)

Though I struggle to forgive
my own imperfections –

the rose's thorns
conceal the lesson
that teaches it to grow.

(xxiv.)

A flash of lightning in the night.

Letting go of the patterns
that narrow my mind –

I follow the thunderbolt's trail
back into the silence.

(xxv.)

I don't want to waste
any more time in uncertainty.
I don't need your approval.

I only hear this 'Yes!' now
that gives its blessings to my heart.

(xxvi.)

As I approach freedom's door,
I pause to remember:

the only way to enter
that space beyond its limit,
is to knock gently.

(xxvii.)

A crow flies through
an open window –

whether I am here or not,
this state of meditation
will never end.

(xxviii.)

Though we've slept many lifetimes,
I'm waking up now
to the dream within the dream…

and beyond that threshold, I can't stop laughing –
there's no such thing as 'awakening'!

(xxix.)

Searching for a place to hide
in this world of pain and loss –

I find paradise waiting
in a breath's
familiar touch.

(xxx.)

All my former lives
are like pages from a book
I don't remember reading.

Lost in the dream-dust of years –
all these words I have forgotten how to say…

(xxxi.)

In truth, I don't mind
if I'm one step behind you –

the next movement I make
will be the only one
that matters.

(xxxii.)

When life makes no sense,
and my heart grieves
for what it's endured –

I take a moment to look within
and find the beauty of others.

(xxxiii.)

I keep forgetting
what I thought I knew.

I've got no need for pointers –

I'm happy just to look at
the silvery light of the moon.

(xxxiv.)

All this poetry
is simply a poor man's attempt
at grasping the ungraspable.

Holding on to these words,
I remember to let go.

(xxxv.)

Turning my heart inside-out,
I feel the soft touch
of the divine.

Even this sensitivity
is a celebration.

(xxxvi.)

From this felled tree stump
small leafy branches grow,
bending softly in the wind.

This trembling in my hands
shows the sadness of my roots.

(xxxvii.)

All your stale criticisms
are stifling the air I breathe.

Whilst you give voice to your faults,
I've simply learnt how to enjoy
the sweet perfume of spring.

(xxxviii.)

Last night, I stole
the moon from the sky.
I left the heavens behind.

This morning when I woke, I felt so slender –
I slipped inside a flower's stem!

(xxxix.)

You mock my attempts
at finding inner peace.

Keep laughing, my friend –

only the jaded find that mountain
where contempt becomes belief.

(xl.)

Watching the way a river flows,
I realise – I can't hold on
to anything.

This world dissolves and forms
in the same moment.

(xli.)

My love, let's lie here together
and give thanks for what we share.

Oh tonight, wherever I touch you –
I feel the abundance
of a field full of flowers.

(xlii.)

I mean what I say,
even when I speak in tongues.

My words are my truth,
and what they express
is the tender frailty of angels.

(xliii.)

The smell of jasmines in the morning
helps me know the simple joy
of just being here at all.

I don't need anyone's permission
to take pleasure in this world.

(xliv.)

Washed clean by autumn rain –
neither in the sky,
nor apart from it –

this unconditional feeling
that releases my sorrow.

(xlv.)

Though I offer them
my kindness –

I can't control
when the orchids
fall.

(xlvi.)

In this realm of light,
there's no need for misery.

Seated beneath the evergreens,
I open a channel in my heart
so that love can find me.

(xlvii.)

I don’t really care
if my dreams come true –

what use do I have for endings,
in this world
of perfect beginnings?

(xlviii.)

There's no recipe for enlightenment.

When you follow the way,
there's no specific step
you need to grasp
but the one you are taking.

(xlix.)

Kissing in the afterglow,
I bring my attention to
the warmth of your breath.

Oh girl, the oneness in you is the same
as the oneness in me!

(1.)

At the core of my being,
there is a space of liberation
no darkness can dim.

Nothing can touch me there
except love itself.

(li.)

I could write ten thousand words
to try and explain 'unity' –

but the only one I need
is the name of the diamond
that's hidden in your heart.

(lii.)

An empty nest
discarded on the ground –

as I touch
the essence of myself,
I leave the nest behind.

(liii.)

In the presence of this
pure arising, it seems:
there is no end to our awakening.

Accomplishing nothing –
we ride the boundless winds.

(liv.)

Removing the barrier
between you and me –

I make all this world a meeting point
for what neither comes
nor goes.

(lv.)

Just as one doubt
creates another,
enlightenment happens
when one trust
becomes nirvana.

(lvi.)

Into my tired mind
I plant these seeds of wisdom.

I won't grieve for what I've lost –
even in the night
the fruit is slowly ripening.

(lvii.)

This butterfly flits by –
shimmering its colour,
and shining starlight in my eyes.

Oh, through this heart-felt connection –
we're one and the same.

(lviii.)

I've created the context
I hold my life in.

Where you see obligations,
I see possibilities
waiting to greet me.

(lix.)

I do not believe
we were made for such sorrow.

Folded tight in the winter,
the sleeping bud does not forget
how to bloom.

(lx.)

In this world of change,
even the most perfect of days
can succumb to the clouds.

In a sudden moment of stillness –
we feel the storm that's coming.

(lxi.)

Anger is the soil
through which my compassion
grows.

The harmony of love
blossoms in everything.

(lxii.)

The voice inside my head
keeps making me its punchline.

Old friend, don't diminish me
with your lies – you've got no idea
what our truth could achieve.

(lxiii.)

The jewel of my heart
has been tested by life's storms.
Still, I've got no time for sadness –

I choose the love that shines
as radiant as suns.

(lxiv.)

I'm no saviour of this world.
I'm just a stranger, celebrating
his song. Listen –

the birds call out this morning
for no-one.

(lxv.)

While it's true I don't really have
a sense of achievement –

the child in my heart
can't stop saying 'thank you'
to the man that I've become.

(lxvi.)

The one I long for
is the one who longs for me.

When the whole of creation
burns with the same soul –
you'll find your true love everywhere.

(lxvii.)

You can't make me feel guilty
for your own stupid 'mistakes'.
There's no such thing as sinning.

When I step onto the path,
I feel the joy in every breath.

(lxviii.)

There's a wisdom that comes
from being intimate
with my vulnerability –

though life has weakened me –
– from these old wounds, lotus flowers grow.

(lxix.)

If the sea
did not trust
the waves –

it would never find
its way to shore.

(lxx.)

Despite appearances,
all of life is unfolding
exactly as it should.

Even in this suffering I sense
the gentle presence of angels.

(lxxi.)

If I could heal the world
with a single poem –

I'd write down
whatever came to mind,
and whisper it to the wind.

(lxxii.)

All my dreams are like
a bubble, floating
on the surface of a lake:

when the bubble bursts,
the water is undisturbed.

(lxxiii.)

In contemplative silence,
I turn within and listen.

In the quiet, it's so clear –
beneath all this pain and loss,
my heart is still unstruck.

(lxxiv.)

True meaning
cannot be caught
in sounds or shapes.

It's the spaces in between
that teach us the mystery.

(lxxv.)

As each grain of sand
contains a world –

to me, it's perfectly clear –
each moment of this life
is a mansion for eternity.

(lxxvi.)

Deep in my knowing,
there is a singular star
that shines the purest light.

If you can't see it with your eyes,
then feel it in your heart.

(lxxvii.)

I can never have
my fill of wine.

If each sip could teach me
to know my worth –
I'd be drunk on the very dregs.

(lxxviii.)

Summer rain came suddenly,
flooding our hearts with tears
from an unseen source.

Beyond all these riverbanks that burst,
there's a limitless ocean.

(lxxix.)

From the outside looking in,
it seems everything diverges
in perfect equality.

If you wanted to give it a name,
you could call it 'divine'.

(lxxx.)

Behind these clouds
birds disappear into the sky.

Ah, yes –
in a moment of illumination,
I see the whole of the path.

(lxxxi.)

Like a star that forms
from the dust of creation –

I keep piling more dirt on my soul.
Oh, but there's no such thing as a stain.
Whenever I polish the mirror, it shines!

(lxxxii.)

This love feels empty
beneath a waning moon.

Alone again in the darkness –
I kneel to the silence,
and the silence kneels back.

(lxxxiii.)

Just as the lotus flowers
disappear beneath the surface –

so there is a secret flower
that opens and closes,
deeper than our eyes can see.

(lxxxiv.)

Manifesting unity –
I bring healing to my heart.

Through these words
I have the power to choose
the life I say I want.

(lxxxv.)

This harmony I feel
is best kept in silence.

Though we all seek the same source –
there are rivers that never meet
the sea.

(lxxxvi.)

This feeling of totality
sends shivers down my spine.

There's no ideal to live up to –
only this willingness
that longs for a connection.

(lxxxvii.)

The sound of birdsong
in the evening
calls me back to myself.

Somewhere in the distance,
a bell is tolling.

(lxxxviii.)

No-one ever told me
I could call myself a poet –

but whose permission do I need
to celebrate
existence?

(lxxxix.)

Abiding timelessly in
this moment, it's easy to see:

all these daffodils I lay my eyes upon
waited a hundred years
just to meet me.

(xc.)

My heart is like a deep dark pool,
hidden in the most secret spot
of some forgotten forest.

So really, who can tell me
what's within it?

(xci.)

I won't deprive myself of love
by getting lost in guilt.

As I release what makes me hurt,
I find the resilience to feel
all of life is moving through me.

(xcii.)

Watching from afar –
this world is reborn,
as it passes away.

With a hundred colours in my eyes,
I simply see what is.

(xciii.)

Thinking back on my life,
I wonder when my purpose
will become clear.

Pausing in the silence,
I feel the universe take a breath.

(xciv.)

Replacing hardship with trust –
I let kindness flood my body
and strengthen my roots.

Now whatever ground I touch,
my whole being flowers there.

(xcv.)

Deep in my loneliness,
I learn to give thanks for
this need to belong.

With no-one to watch me,
I turn this prayer into a dance.

(xcvi.)

I live in the awareness
of befriending each moment.

Why should I fear the night?
Without it, how would I see
the stars?

(xcvii.)

Paradise is hidden
in the eyes of unknowing.

Like moonlight reflecting
on the sea – this distance I travel
between heaven and earth.

(xcviii.)

There is a garden of truth
the world can never find.

It's not charted on any maps.
As soon as you step foot in it –
it disappears!

(xcix.)

All of life is divine,
from the depths unto the heights.

In this timeless valley
of one thousand-petalled flowers –
I bow to nothing.

(c.)

Oh, if only
I could abide here
forever:

the ecstatic heart
of creation!

## About the Author

C.W. Blackburn is a mystic poet, currently living in Bournemouth, a seaside town on the south coast of England. In 2011, at the age of 24, he started undergoing a series of peak experiences, which led to a gradual shift in his perception from the material to the spiritual. After a return of mental health struggles in his later twenties, he began reading into the wisdom teachings of the major world religions and spiritual traditions, which is the influence and inspiration for his poetry. His other collections include *Where Words Are Yet To Be Spoken: Poems for Presence*, *Disorder: 23 Poems About Mental Health*, and *The Gospel of Silence: Poems for the Living One.*

C.W. Blackburn can be contacted via Sundara Poetry Press at sundarapoetry@gmail.com.

***Also available by C.W. Blackburn***

## Where Words Are Yet To Be Spoken: Poems for Presence

*'If you want to know where I've been – I went under, I went within…' – Hope*

In his first collection, mystic poet C.W. Blackburn takes us on a heartfelt and imaginative journey into the hidden realms of the spiritual. Following the recurrence of struggles with his mental health, Blackburn explores the themes of infinity and eternity, silence and space, stillness and healing – culminating in the ecstatic realisation of the love and divinity that lies not outside of us, but awaits within.

Rooted in the presence of this greater potential we all share, these are poems of creativity and vision – a love letter to the poetic tradition and human spirit, celebrating beauty, truth and the mysterious question at the heart of our existence: the sheer miracle and strange wonder of what it means to be anything at all.

*Praise for 'Where Words Are Yet To Be Spoken':*

'Beautiful poems born of struggle that touch the soul with an invitation to live deeper.' – Tim Freke, Author – *The Mystery Experience,* and *Jesus & The Lost Goddess* (co-authored with Peter Gandy)

'An exploration into Being that delights the heart…' – Shruti Bakshi, Author and Poet – *HeartWords: Mystic Poems*

'Life-affirming.' – John Foster, Playwright and Screenwriter

'Poems of remembrance, longing, and celebration…' – Fiona Robertson, Author – *The Dark Night of the Soul: A Journey from Absence to Presence*

'Unique and magical…' – Samantha SolBright Rodriguez, Author – *Living as Pure Love: Returning To Our True Essence*

'A great gift…' – Rashani Réa, Author – *Beyond Brokenness,* and *Go Slowly, Breathe and Smile* (co-authored with Thich Nhat Hanh)

## Disorder: 23 Poems About Mental Health

*'How long can we endure these shadows alone? This uneasiness in our hearts that no-one knows how to cure?' – Trauma*

In this specially themed collection, poet C.W. Blackburn examines the cycles of generational trauma through the lens of various mental health conditions. Speaking from his own experience with anxiety and OCD, Blackburn evokes the reality of living with a mental health disorder by taking the reader directly into the thought patterns involved in each condition. At once illuminating and poignant, *Disorder* is a work designed to raise awareness for mental health during a time of increasing instability.

50% of the proceeds earned by the author for this book will be donated to mental health charities in the United Kingdom, with the aim of aiding those in need of support and empowerment.

*Praise for 'Disorder':*

'These poems are not 'about' mental health conditions, but rather a direct and deeply personal expression of what it is like to be in 'the headspaces that other lives get trapped in.' Many of us, myself included, live our lives coloured by some combination of anxiety, trauma, depression or other kinds of psychological suffering. As C.W. Blackburn shares, living with such states can be an intensely lonely and overwhelming experience. Simply knowing that we are not alone – that other people's minds also do what ours does – can be profoundly relieving. I wholeheartedly recommend these poems both to those who are familiar with this territory and to those who aren't. Thank you, C.W. Blackburn, for your simple yet profoundly resonant poetry.' – Fiona Robertson, Author – *The Dark Night of the Soul: A Journey from Absence to Presence*

## The Gospel of Silence: Poems for the Living One

*'So, this is the Second Coming…' – Faith*

In his fourth collection, mystic poet C.W. Blackburn explores the idea of 'oneness' in a story that unfolds on three different levels of consciousness, as a collective shift in perception re-awakens humanity to its own highest potential.

Starting with the prophetic proclamation of The Second Coming, 'The Christ' returns not only as a man, but also as the Divine Light manifested within each soul. Resurrecting Sophia, his ancient Goddess of Wisdom, the two march onwards towards the battlegrounds of eternity to face the monstrous Beast – the terrifying embodiment of the human ego and its bitter legacy. Meanwhile, in another time and place, a solitary poet struggles to find his voice again after suffering a heart-breaking injury that has rendered him speechless.

Inspired by Gnostic Christianity, yoga philosophy, Tantric Buddhism, and the prophetic books of William Blake, *The Gospel of Silence: Poems for the Living One* is a call to unity during times of increasing division and a radical new re-interpretation of the universal truth at the heart of all spirituality.

'C.W. Blackburn's *Gospel of Silence* is an inspired work of gentle, everyday revelation that returns us to the wisdom of our hearts.' – Mike Jenkins, Poet & Meditation Teacher, *heartofpresence.co.uk*

Printed in Great Britain
by Amazon

22594160R00067